Note from the Author:

Thank you for joining me on this adventure of becoming a Leading Lady! I believe that every young girl has a heart of gold and it is our job to chip away at the rough edges, until we discover the richness their lives have to offer. It's like a miner. When they're mining, they know that what they see isn't what they'll ultimately end up with. They dig, dig some more and chip away at the rock until they discover the gold hiding deep within. That is what I hope this study will do for each and every young lady who reads it. I hope that their character would be chipped away at until all that is left is a Heart of Gold!

Sincerely,

Vonae Deyshawn

How to use this study:

Throughout the workbook, there are several elements to each session. You will find a pre-activity, the lesson, a short story segment, a reflection/journaling piece, and a scrapbooking page. The scrapbook page is a fun place where each young lady can visually place her thoughts, ideas and dreams for the future.

We would encourage an adult to walk through the lesson portion of each segment, but it is not required. The best results we've experienced have come from intentional studying, application and completion. Each activity placed within a session helps to build off of the lesson, bringing real life situations in order to apply the 8 chosen principles.

If you have any questions during your journey through the study, please feel free to contact us at Contact@VonaeDeyshawn.com . We hope you will enjoy Volume One of Heart of Gold!

~The Virtue Media Team

Session One

Session One

Pre-Activity

Take a moment and think about your closest group of friends. Got your list? Good! Below is a sketch of four girls. Imagine that they are you and your girlfriends. Name each one, but don't think too much about the order in which they appear. After you've named each one, go back and describe them using only adjectives. The goal is to describe how you view them and yourself. At this point you're probably wondering why . . . You'll have to wait to find out.

Session One

Traits of a Leader

Everyone looks up to someone . . . Why Can't that someone be you?

Directions: Circle the word that completes each statement best.

1. A leader is someone who {inspires, tells, watches} others to:
   - Take action.
   - Dream.
   - Go above and beyond.

That's right! Leaders **inspire** others to do something that they wouldn't do on their own. They motivate their friends, support causes and help others just because it's the right thing to do.

Some inspiring people might include Oprah Winfrey, Katy Perry, Britt Nicole, Hilary Clinton, Jamie Grace and the list could go on!

Take a moment and think about someone who inspires you. What is it about that person that makes you want to be different, to change?

_____
_____
_____

2. A leader is someone who {criticizes, encourages, teases} others to:
   - Bring change.
   - Make others **feel** better.
   - Make a difference.

Encouraging others is one of the greatest things anyone can do. It's simply finding the best in someone and then telling them about it. Leaders make others feel better about themselves and the things they can accomplish through compliments, words of support and pointing out the good they have to offer this world.

3. A leader **shows confidence**.
   - Not easily changed or convinced.
   - Has a clear understanding what they want for their life.
   - Has a positive self-image.
   - Are comfortable in their own skin.

4. A Leader **pursues excellence**.
   - Never settles for less than the best.
   - Doesn't just do the bare minimum.

LEADERSHIP VALUES	How am I reflecting these values in my everyday life?
INSPIRE	
ENCOURAGE	
SHOW CONFIDENCE	
PURSUES EXCELLENCE	

Time is neutral and does not change things. With courage and initiative, leaders change things. –Jesse Jackson

If your actions inspire others to dream more, learn more, do more and become more, you are a leader. –John Quincy Adams

Session One

Explore

I sat in class, doodling on the handout Mr. Schumacher had been babbling on and on about for the past hour. His scruffy beard and sun-kissed face bobbed around the classroom demanding that we "Become leaders, not followers!" This was his usual enthusiasm. Every message he delivered from his imaginary stage at the front of the classroom was as he put it "vital for our lives." He even managed to smile all the way through them. Usually, I enjoyed his little tirades but today, today I was not in the mood. To be honest, he was seriously starting to get on my nerves with all this talk. Like really, who doesn't know that they should be a leader, that they should make their own decisions? Why did he feel the need to beat us over the head with something that everyone already knows? It's common sense!

"Madison, Madison?" I heard a voice hiss from behind me. Turning reluctantly, I already knew who it was. It was the same voice

I'd been hearing for years. The voice that had lived next door to me since I waddled around the house in *Huggies* Pull-Up diapers. It was the infamous voice of my partner in crime. The voice that had earned me five detentions in Mr. Schumacher's class to date and school had only been in for two months!

"What?" I whispered, staring at my brown eyed friend, her dark bangs falling across her face.

"So Tristan's having a party tonight. I hear it's going to be epic! Wanna go?"

"I . . . I don't know. Remember what happened the last time we went to one of your so called "epic" parties? Besides, you know I can't. It's a school night."

"Oh come on. Don't be so lame. It's not like you <u>need</u> to do any homework or study or anything. Your GPA is like a four point nine."

"You obviously know that's not the reason," I shot back, rolling my eyes.

"Oh my gosh! Just sneak out. Your mom goes to bed at like 9 o'clock," she insisted, her aggravation turning her voice from a whisper to a high pitched command.

"Madison and Jessica," Mr. Schumacher boomed from the front of the classroom, making my heart almost pound out of my chest. He wasn't the least bit scary, its just that my mom promised that if I received one more detention from him that she'd have me shipped off to an all girls private school. "Apparently," he continued, waving his arms above his head in giant swirls. "Your conversation is more important that mine. Would you like to come up here and teach the class? You obviously think whatever you're talking about is more relevant."

"No thank . . ." I began before I was cut off by a "sure!" as Jessica jumped from her seat and sauntered to the front of the room.

"This will be a cinch," she added as she flailed her arms and started impersonating our teacher's every move.

The class went wild as she paced back and forth; making a mockery of everything he had just spent the last hour trying to get across. I didn't even know she was listening well enough to do a perfect rendition of his lesson. One thing Jessica had been gifted with at a young age was an immense IQ which came with an equally massive attitude. She always had a comment, opinion, comeback, or some smart aleck response that made even the most confident person clam up and run for cover.

Mr. Schumacher stood off to the side of his desk, leaning uncomfortably on a stack of papers. I noticed that his right hand was balled into a fist and that his usually cheery face, no longer had any trace of sunlight. Instead of his normal calm demeanor, he was glaring at Jessica, his eyes ablaze. It truly looked like he might explode or maybe go running out of the classroom, tears streaming down his face. It was then when it hit me. I felt bad for him. Not just bad, but sick. Why would he let her continue to humiliate him in front of his entire class? It was just down right awful.

This went on for a full ten minutes until the bell finally sounded. With a grin and a bow, Jessica dismissed the class and returned to her desk to grab her things, not even bothering to look at our teacher who stood there in disbelief. I sat there equally dumbfounded; Disgusted at what had just unfolded. I watched as Mr. Schumacher grabbed his briefcase, shoved the papers that were scattered across his desk into it, and storm out of the room; slamming the door behind him.

"That guy is so uptight," Jessica asserted as she picked up her binder and tote. "Like seriously, did you see how upset he got? He needs to get a life. Hello, are you coming?" She demanded, waving her hand in front of my face.

Was she really expecting an answer, some sort of praise or handclap? Honestly, the last thing I wanted to do was go anywhere with her. Was she serious? He was the uptight one? I scrambled to my feet, picking up my bags and dragged myself behind her, trying to shake off the immense feeling that my best friend was not at all who I thought she was. She continued talking as I fell into place beside her but it wasn't the same. I pretended to listen as she went on and on about what we should wear tonight to the party, but I wasn't so sure I wanted to go to. After that little tirade, I wasn't even sure I wanted to be her friend.

"See you tonight," she sang over her shoulder as she disappeared into the crowd of students a smug smile plastered on her face.

"Yeah tonight," I grumbled, hoisting my tote onto my shoulder and heading towards my next class.

Share Your Thoughts

In the story, Madison sees her best friend acting out in class. While Madison wants to be loyal to her friendship with Jessica, she knows that her behavior is unacceptable. According to what we know are traits of a leader, would you consider Madison a leader? Why or why not? What are some pieces of advice that you could give Madison to help her become more of a leader?

SCRAPBOOK YOUR THOUGHTS

Session Two

Session Two

Pre-Activity

Self-Image

For this activity, I want you to think of someone who seems to be super confident to you. Why do you think they're so confident? What do they do that makes them seem that way? In the frame above, do your best to sketch them. (If you are horrible at drawing like me, you can draw some items that reflect them instead of a full person). Below, briefly describe the person and what makes them "appear" to be so great.

_____
_____

Session Two

Building a Positive Self-Image

"To wish you were someone else is to waste the person you are."

1. Take a moment and think about all the things you know or have heard that shows someone has a good self-image. What are some of those things? In your own words, what is self-image?

Self-image is the personal view we have of ourselves. It's what we think about ourselves, how we perceive our appearance, and how we choose our friends.

So the question is how do we build a positive self-image?

2. A positive self-image is built by understanding that we aren't {smart, perfect, capable}.

If you picked **perfect**, you're right! A person with a positive self-image knows it's okay to be themselves because no matter how hard they try, it's impossible to be perfect. Knowing that, they can accept themselves for who they are.

- No one is perfect and if they tell you differently, run!
- Stop criticizing yourself, it's okay to just be you!
- Practice positive criticism. If you see something could be improved, address the problem and then come up with possible solutions.

3. A positive self-image is built by recognizing what you've done well or have accomplished.

- Don't be afraid to praise yourself.
- Accept compliments by teachers or peers. If someone says you do something well, accept it and allow yourself to be praised.

4. A positive self-image is built by choosing your {parents, siblings, friends} wisely.

- Choose friends that are going to push you to do and be better than what you already are.
- Hang out with people who uplift you, not put you down.
- Remember that a friendship is not a <u>competition</u>. It's the opportunity to combine the traits gifted to each and every one of us to make a difference in the lives of others.

Things to remember to build your self-image:

- **Accept who you are!**
- **Stop comparing yourself to others.**
- **Learn to love yourself and treat yourself well.**
- **Be comfortable with your body.**

You are unique and were created with a special purpose in mind. Not one of us is alike because we were knitted together in a special way that would allow us to accomplish the plan set forth for our lives. No one can be you and you can't be anyone else. Love the person you are!

Session Two

Explore

Self-Image Check-Up

In order to make a change in your self-image, you must first know how strong or weak yours currently is and that's what you're going to do right now. As a part of your explore activities this week, you will take a quiz that will show you where you rank when it comes to self-image. No one will see your results, so be sure to answer honestly.

1. I'm okay with making mistakes. I know we learn by failing and if I never fail, how will I learn?

a) never b) sometimes c) always

2. What others think of me means a lot. It really affects how I feel as a person.

a) never b) sometimes c) always

3. I say sorry a lot and it's mostly because I don't like asking for help.

a) never b) sometimes c) always

4. I'm really upset with myself when I do something stupid or wrong.

a) never b) sometimes c) always

5. I would do something that I know is wrong in order to fit in.

a) never b) sometimes c) always

6. When I look in the mirror, I only see the bad things about myself.

a) never b) sometimes c) always

7. Sometimes I wish I were smarter and prettier.

a) never b) sometimes c) always

8. I'm okay with feeling emotions; anger, sadness, jealousy, happiness, etc.

a) never b) sometimes c) always

9. I'm okay with asking my friends and family for help when I need it.

a) never b) sometimes c) always

10. I'm okay with being alone sometimes.

a) never b) sometimes c) always

Results: Follow the key below, adding each answer to see where you rank.

1. a:1 b:2 c:3   6. a:3 b:2 c:1

2. a:3 b:2 c:1   7. a:3 b:2 c:1

3. a:3 b:2 c:1   8. a:1 b:2 c:3

4. a:3 b:2 c:1   9. a:1 b:2 c:3

5. a:3 b:2 c:1   10. a:1 b:2 c:3

10-15: Needs Work

You base a lot of how you feel about yourself on how others view you. You hate making mistakes and take yourself very seriously. If you could change things about yourself, it would be your looks. Sometimes you have a hard time not comparing yourself to others and you don't like being alone. Overall, you know you could be more confident, you just don't know how to get there yet.

20-16 points: So-So

You have a good sense of who you are but sometimes you wish you could change a few things. People don't usually affect the way you see yourself but in certain situations they can. You tend to make good decisions on your own and pick friends that are a lot like you. You're never alone but if you had to be, you'd find something to do. You enjoy being with your friends and family and look to them for advice. Overall,

30-21 points: Great!

You have a very healthy self-image. You know exactly who you are and don't find it hard to show it. People don't tend to change your mind on things, which sometimes makes you look stubborn. You're comfortable doing things alone like reading, watching a movie, writing a journal, etc. You value your friendships and the advice they offer you. You know how to filter good and bad advice in order to make yourself a better person.

Session Two

Explore

"Good night honey," my mother called from the hall.

"Good night," I responded robotically. It was our nightly routine. She would call out her good night, which was my signal for bed. Usually, I would go right to sleep, not tonight. The palms of my hands felt clammy and my stomach was balled into knots as I waited to hear the click of her bedroom door.

My mom made it a priority to go to bed super early since she liked to go running before dawn and see my father off before one of his "busy" days at the office. I sat in the dark, shifting uneasily in my royal blue dress and flip flops that at the moment were crammed under my oversized down comforter. It was 9:15 and Jessica was supposed to be picking me up around 9:25. Once again she had talked me into going to one of her "epic" parties. I agreed to go under one condition, that she admit how rude she was today in class.

At first she refused, calling me "uptight," but when she saw I was serious, she apologized and swore the next time she saw Mr. Schumacher she would beg for his forgiveness. That was something I couldn't wait to see.

The hall light finally turned off and I heard the click of my mother's door as she settled in for the night. Butterflies danced violently in my stomach as I slid from underneath the blanket and tiptoed to my window. Our house was two-stories but ever since I was little, my parents had kept an emergency ladder attached outside of my room in case of a fire. To Jessica, everything was a fire so I learned to use it quite well. If there were ever actually a fire, my parents could be sure I would get out of the house just fine. Climbing down, I reached the lawn and dashed across it, running at full speed to the cluster of hedges that surrounded our home. Through the bushes, I could see the headlights of her car as it idled on the next street. How she managed to go out every night and not be tired at school every day was beyond me. Shooting from the bushes, I raced to her car; breathing a sigh of relief as I sank into her leather seats.

"It's about time," she shot, sending the car in motion with a quick jerk. "I thought I was going to have to come and ring your doorbell."

"Yeah right," I retorted. "You wouldn't dare."

"Oh I wouldn't?" she smirked, turning onto the main street. "So are you ready for an awesome party?"

"Um, I guess. I just hope I don't get caught. My parents would murder me."

"Don't be such a baby. They would never do such a thing. Besides, you're their only child." She laughed as she pulled into a blue and white two-story home.

The lawn was littered with cars and red cups as Jessica maneuvered onto the curb. Parking, we climbed out of the car and made our way up to the house. The front door was open and the sound of music came pulsating out of it, accompanied by flashing strobe lights. Jessica ran ahead, jumping through the door in a grand fashion and waving her hands high above her head to the music. The white lights flashed on her tight red mini dress making her look like she was dancing in slow motion. A few guys walked up to her and started chatting her up as she moved to the beat. One of them, a tall muscular guy with a serious tan and dark hair put his arm around her shoulder. Winking at his friend who responded by punching him in the arm.

"Of course I didn't come alone." Jessica was saying as I walked up.

"And who are you?" asked the shorter, less attractive of the two guys.

"I'm Madison," I answered, cringing from the stench that floated from his mouth to my face.

"She's a little young to be at a party isn't she?" the tall guy asked, laughing as he pulled Jessica closer.

"She's not too young," Jessica replied, giving me a face, wanting me to lie and say that I was. "She's a senior."

"A senior, I've never seen a senior dress like that," the tall guy frowned. "Have you Jason?"

"Nope," snorted Jason, giving me the once over before falling into a fit of laughter.

Jessica and the tall guy joined in, laughing like he'd told some ultra hilarious joke. I stood there in the doorway, feeling like I was twelve inches tall. I wanted to cry. Run away. Be anywhere but standing here feeling like a piece of worthless trash. What made things worse was that Jessica hadn't taken up for me, no instead she was standing there laughing at me too. Before I knew what was happening, I was out the door and running through the crowded front yard. I didn't care that it was late at night, or that I lived three blocks away. I ran as fast as my legs would carry me; taking off my flip-flops and tucking them under my arm. Heat surged from my head and I could feel tears streaming from my eyes and burning my face as I ran against the wind.

Finally, I made it to my house. Instead of going to my window, I stopped and stood on the front lawn, breathing heavily. Wiping my eyes with my stupid blue dress I put my flip-flops back on and actually looked at the house for the first time. All the lights had been turned on and I could see my mom and dad, sitting in the living room, staring at the front door.

Share Your Thoughts

In the next segment of the story, Madison makes a series of bad decisions. Think about her decisions and then of a time when you made a bad decision(s) of your own. What was it and how did things turn out for you?

SCRAPBOOK YOUR THOUGHTS

Session Three

Session Three

Pre-Activity

Dependability

For this activity, you will read each statement and then choose the answer that best reflects your opinion.

1. If my parents ask me to do something like clean my room, I do it right away.

A. Of course   B. I might complain a little, but it will get done.

C. Never

2. People can trust me to keep secrets.

A. Yep.   B. I might tell someone else and make sure they wont tell anyone else.   C. Not really

3. My parents and teachers count on me to do special jobs.

A. They ask all the time.   B. Not usually.   C. Never

4. I tend to keep the same group of friends and we tell each other everything.

A. Yep, it's great.   B. Sometimes I don't like hanging out with the same people.   C. Not really

5. When someone asks me to do something, I make sure I go out of my way to make it great.

A. Always   B. I do exactly what I'm asked.   C. I just try to get it done.

6. I tend to lose things that I have.

A. Always   B. Sometimes   C. Never

7. I give a lot of advice because people usually ask me.

A. Always   B. Not really   C. Never

8. It aggravates me when people ask me for help. I don't understand why they can't do it themselves.

A. Never   B. Yeah sometimes.   C. Always

Results:

Mostly A's: You are a very dependable person and this isn't a mistake. You work really hard to make sure you keep your word and to make sure people can count on you. Be careful because this may cause you to burn out. Never be afraid to say no to a task if you feel like you can't handle it. You will still be seen as dependable, but you will be able to do the fewer things better than trying to do many things "so-so."

Mostly B's: People tend to ask you to do things for them and generally trust you with important tasks. You like helping others, but sometimes you just don't want to. There's nothing wrong with saying no. Just make sure you're saying no for the right reasons or people may start to see you as selfish.

Mostly C's: You seem to lack dependability. People usually don't come to you for advice because they're afraid that whatever they say may get around to others. You also may find it hard to make and maintain friends, which sometimes leaves you frustrated and alone. Work at volunteering for tasks and doing them well. This will start to build a relationship with the person you do it for and will in turn produce new relationships.

Session Three

Becoming a dependable person

To give your word but not be trusted to carry it out is a waste of breath.

1. Before we start, I want you to picture yourself sitting on the curb outside of your school. It's a typical Tuesday afternoon but you stayed late because you had to make up work from the day you were home sick with the flu. You called your parent during lunch and told them that you would need to stay and they agreed to pick you up at 5:00pm. Fast forward to now. You look down at your cell phone and read that it's 5:45pm. Not only are they late, but you desperately need to use the restroom, you're starving, and it's about fifty degrees outside. How are you feeling as you sit on your imaginary curb?

2. So what is dependability?

- The assurance that someone can **count** on you to get the job done.
- Keeping private information {private, public, sort of to yourself}.
- Being {busy, available, uninterested}.
- Saying that you'll do something and then actually **doing** it.

    Answers: Private and available

3. Why is it important for leaders to learn to be dependable?

    A. Dependability builds {conversation, friendships, enemies}.
- If people can count on you, they're more likely to value you as a friend.

        I. Think about someone you call a close friend. What about them makes you want to open up to them?

        _____
        _____

        II. Think about someone who you thought was your friend, what about them made you change your mind?

        _____
        _____

    B. Dependability builds **trust**.
- If a friend can trust you, they're more likely to come to you with a personal problem or to seek your advice.

    C. People will see you as {irresponsible, responsible, nonchalant}.
- If you are dependable, people will see you as responsible; providing you with special positions of leadership and projects to complete.

4. How do we become dependable? By,

    i. Keeping our **word**.
    ii. **Showing** up.
    iii. Being on **time**.
    iv. Doing what we're **asked**.

Session Three

Explore

My heart was pounding out of my chest as I made my way up the lawn. My parents were probably going to rip me a new one if I walked through that front door, but at this point, what choice did I have? It's not like I could sneak through my window and come downstairs saying "Hey guys, what's going on?" They obviously knew I wasn't home. Every step I took, getting closer to the door made my stomach sink into my shoes. The wet grass crunched beneath my shoes making more noise than I would have liked. Stepping onto the porch, I turned the knob of the door and walked into the living room.

"Where have you been young lady!" my mother shouted, jumping from the plush mocha leather sofa and waving her arms above her head. "You'd better have a real good story."

"Relax honey, I'll handle this," my father said calmly, pulling my mother back down to her seat. "Have a seat Madison," he smiled grimly. I sat in on the love seat across the room, my stomach balling into a thousand knots. "So," he started between sips of his coffee. "Where were you? We've been waiting for over a hour."

That was the thing about my dad. While my mom was great, my dad never got angry. I honestly don't think he knows how to and that's what makes getting in trouble by him awful. His calm demeanor always made me feel the worse. It was like they were so perfect and I was the child that just couldn't get it right. I mean I could get it right, it's just the people I hang out with that make me get it wrong. They or should I say she was the cause of most my riffs with my parents. Not like that's going to be a problem anymore. With how she treated me tonight, I could care less if I ever talked to her again.

"I . . . I," I stuttered, trying to find a way to get out of trouble. He just looked at me and shook his head. "I went to a party with Jessica," I sighed, grinding my shoe into the rug.

"On a school night?" my mother shouted, "Are you out of your mind? Did you forget our last conversation? That's it, I'm so sick of this. That girl Jessica is bad news."

"I know," I mumbled, picking at my jeans.

"That's not far Amanda," my father frowned at my mom. "Madison has her own brain and therefore she can make her own decisions. We can't blame Jessica for what Madison chooses to do."

"But dad, she made me," I pleaded.

"She made you?" my dad repeated, looking confused. "Did she threaten you or something?"

"Um no."

"Madison, we're so disappointed in you. You need to start taking responsibility for your own actions and not blame others for things you decide to do. Your mother and I expect way more from you and it's time that you start showing it. We try to trust you, but every time we do, you do something that makes us not trust you."

"But dad you can trust me!" I shrieked, shocked at his words.

"Apparently not honey."

Share Your Thoughts

In the third part of the story, Madison gets caught sneaking out, disappointing her parents. Think about a time when you did something that left someone disappointed in you. How did it make you feel? How would you go back and change what you did?

SCRAPBOOK YOUR THOUGHTS

Session Four

Session Four

R-E-S-P-E-C-T

"If you find it hard to respect others, the least you can do is respect yourself."

5. We've all heard the infamous respect song and if you haven't, you should take a minute to listen to it. Respect is the key ingredient that makes things happen for you, or to you. It's what makes people feel valued and appreciated. So the question is, are you respectful?

    Before we begin discussing what respect is, let's first explore disrespect. We don't have to go far to see someone being disrespectful. For some of us, that someone is us. Let me be clear, that doesn't mean you're a bad person; it just means we have some work to do.

    So what is disrespect?

6. Disrespect is:
    A) Treating others {poorly, good, nicely}.
    - This usually happens when we get the idea that we're better than others. Sorry to tell you, but we are all created equally no matter our color, age, or social class.

    B) **Talking** back to authority figures. (Ex. Parents, teachers, coaches, any adult).
    - Having a response or snickering when asked to do something.

C) Not {liking, following, hearing} directions.

- Gives the attitude that you're above the rules, therefore you don't have to follow the same instructions everyone else has to.

D) **Destroying** the property of someone else.

- Having little or no value for the things of others.

If you answered poorly and following, you are correct! Do you possess any of the qualities? I sure hope not. Lets look at what it means to be respectful.

7. Respect is:

A) **Valuing** others.
- You understand that everyone is created equally so you treat them that way, regardless if they are someore you know and like or not.

B) Doing what you're **asked**.

- Not the third time, but the first!

C) Taking {control, care} of things that belong to others.

- If someone let's you borrow something, you make sure to return it in the same condition you received it.

D) Not **talking** back.

- Whether you agree about what someone is saying to you or not, you know when it's best to keep quiet. This doesn't mean you are a push over. You just know there are better ways to handle a situation than to talk back.

Session Four

Explore

The next few days were a blur. I went to school but it felt like I was floating in the clouds. I didn't feel like myself at all. My parents talked to me, but I could tell they were still disappointed. As far as Jessica, she called but I ignored her, giving the excuse that I was grounded whenever she asked why I couldn't talk. She would give her usual "that sucks" and that would be the end of the conversation. No "I'm sorry I got you in trouble and made fun of you." She didn't even mention the night of the party with the guys. It was clear she didn't care. The only time I had to see her was during Mr. Schumacher's class, which consequently wasn't his class anymore. He had been replaced by a "permanent substitute" as they put it because he had a family emergency he had to attend to. We all knew exactly what emergency he had.

The only good thing that came from us having a replacement was the creation of a seating chart. In order to learn our names, the sub made us sit in alphabetical order which meant Jessica would be across the room since her last name began with an "R" and mine with a "B." It was probably the best thing that ever happened to me. In the past three days, I was actually able to meet new people and be myself. I was so used to Jessica being the center of attention that I never knew I could be fine without her, but surprisingly I was.

Share Your Thoughts

In the next part of the story, we find Madison reflecting on what happened between her and Jessica. Would you say Jessica is a respectable person? What about Madison? Who is someone in your life that you feel treats you like Jessica treats Madison? After our lesson, how do you feel about your "friendship?"

SCRAPBOOK YOUR THOUGHTS

Session Five

Session Five

Pre-Activity

Manners Quiz

1. When you receive a gift card for your birthday from your grandmother, how do you respond?

A. Go shopping right away!

B. Call to say thank you.

C. Think to yourself, "That was nice of her," but wait to say thank you at Christmas dinner. After all, she sends you gifts all the time and that'd be an awful lot of phone calls and you wouldn't want to talk to her that often, she's boring.

2. You're at a restaurant for family day with your parents and your cell phone rings. It's your best friend Jamie. You...

A. Apologize for even having your phone on, turn it off, and go back to spending time with your family.

B. Say "Sorry," and answer your phone.

C. Take the call. After all, why would your parents mind - it's your best friend calling.

3. Dinner is finished with your family, and you notice a cute guy but you didn't put on any make-up and you desperately need some lipgloss or eye shadow. You...

A. Excuse yourself to the bathroom to freshen up.

B. Quickly apply some gloss at the table and leave it at that.

C. Pull out your make-up, apply your lipgloss and mascara.

4. You're attending a birthday party for your friend's little sister. Do you bring anything?

A. Yes. You go to her favorite store and buy her a giftcard for $20, two shirts, and a necklace.

B. No, I wouldn't expect her to bring me anything. It's not like we're friends.

C. A card should be good enough.

5. Your hairdresser just gave you the best haircut of his life. How much do you tip her?

A. I'm supposed to tip my stylist?

B. My mom already pays him enough.

C. An extra $10. I really appreciate his hard work.

6. You've just finished watching a movie and feel the strong urge to use the bathroom. When you arrive there is a huge line and you have to wait at least five minutes. Your bladder feels like it's going to explode as you sway back and forth. Behind you, you can hear a small child whining to their mother that they have to go really bad. The little girl looks to be about five years old and tears are streaming down her face. Finally it's your turn to go. You . . .

A. It depends how bad she's crying.

B. You feel really bad, but hey you had to wait so they can too.

C. You politely turn to the mom and tell her that they can go.

7. You're trying on a bunch of clothes in the dressing room of Macy's but you only choose a few clothes to purchase. What does your dressing room usually look like when you leave?

A. Like a tornado just passed through.

B. Nice and neat. All of the clothes you passed on are hanging neatly on their hangers.

C. Your room is empty because you returned the clothes to the dressing room attendant.

8. You borrow one of your best friend's favorite movies to watch on a boring Friday night. How do you return it to her?

A. You have it wiped with alcohol and placed into its case and back to her the very next day.

B. You wait for her to ask for it back. That way, if she forgets, you can watch it a few more times.

C. You'll give it back to her the next time you see her, even though you accidentally dropped it on the floor and it got scratched. She won't notice.

Calculate Your Results:

1. A: 5 pts   B: 15 pts   C: 10 pts

2. A: 15 pts   B: 10 pts   C: 5 pts

3. A: 15 pts   B: 10 pts   C: 5 pts

4. A: 15 pts   B: 5 pts   C: 10 pts

5. A: 10 pts   B: 5 pts   C: 15 pts

6. A: 10 pts   B: 5 pts   C: 15 pts

7. A: 5 pts   B: 10 pts   C: 15 pts

8. A: 15 pts   B: 10 pts   C: 5 pts

100-120 points GREAT MANNERS

80-99 points YOU HAVE MANNERS SOMETIMES

79- below YOUR MANNERS NEED WORK

Session five

Manners . . . Who needs them?

"Some look at manners as a thing of the past, but if you don't have any you can forget about your future."

1. **Read the following list of scenarios. Without overthinking it, write your first reactions in the space below.**
   - Someone drops money.
   - Someone slides through the door as it closes causing it to slam in your face.
   - A kid at lunch reaches into your food and steals a chip.
   - Someone texts you a rude message.

*So who needs Manners?

2. **{Some people, adults, everyone}!**

That's right, everyone needs manners!!

- <u>**You.**</u>
- <u>Your friends at school</u>.
- <u>Your teachers</u>.
- <u>Your parents</u>.
- And_____. (You can fill in the blank here. Yes, they're included too).

*Just imagine how better the world would be if even a few of these people showed manners.

* **What are manners?**

    3. Manners are the things we do to be . . .

    - {Rude, Polite, Stubborn}
    - **Caring**
    - {Respectful, Disrespectful, Mean}
    - **Honest**

    With others.

    Answers: Polite and Respectful

    4. Manners are the <u>customs</u> and <u>traditions</u> of a society.
    A. List at least 5 standard manners in the American culture. I'll give you one.
    1. Saying excuse me when you need to pass someone.
    2.
    3.
    4.
    5.

    B. What are some manners that you may practice that could be different from the American culture?

    1. Kissing on the cheek while greeting.
    2.
    3.
    4.
    5.

5. Manners are also used to make people feel <u>comfortable</u>.

By using manners, people know what to expect from you, which gives a level of comfort. If I know it's bad manners to talk with my mouth full but do it anyway, there's a good chance the people eating with me are going to feel uncomfortable. I guarantee they won't want to see my mashed up food falling out of my mouth as I ramble on.

6. Manners can also be used to make people <u>uncomfortable</u>.

Have you ever heard of the phrase, "Kill them with kindness?" It simply means that no matter how someone else acts or treats you, be nice to them anyway. Unfortunately, we live in a world where everyone is not going to like you and that's okay. Maintaining your level of respect, kindness and politeness will go a long way and probably even make them uncomfortable.

Reflect

As we conclude this lesson, how do you think you're doing in the manners department?

_____
_____
_____
_____
_____
_____

Explore

Practice: Over the next few days, be intentional about practicing manners. In the chart below, keep record of when you've used a manner and then list it. Each time you use a good manner, have the person receiving the action sign in the box for you.

Manners Chart

ACTION	DATE	PERSON RECEIVING ACTION	SIGNATURE

Session Five

Explore

It was finally the weekend and my parents decided to let me off the hook early. We talked and I assured them that I was done with hanging out with Jessica. I think they could see that I was serious, so they agreed to let me go to the mall with a friend I'd known since eighth grade but hadn't really talked to much since going to high school. I waited on the couch for her to come, sipping some fresh squeezed orange juice and watching a re-run of my favorite show. My phone buzzed across the coffee table, signaling the receiving of a text. It was short and sweet, "I'm here." I gathered my things, shouting over my shoulder to my mom that I was leaving and would be home for dinner. Climbing into the car, I was excited to be out of the house and finally doing something.

"Hey pretty lady," Dina smiled as I buckled in. "Where to first?"

"Hmm, how about Amber's Collections?"

"That works for me," she sang, backing out of the driveway and heading towards the mall.

We arrived in a short amount of time and headed towards our destination. The mall was buzzing with students, carrying shopping bags, drinking coffee, and just hanging out. Deep down I hoped that I wouldn't run into Jessica who loved coming to the mall; it was just not a conversation I was ready to have. We browsed through my favorite store, picking out outfits and taking turns modeling them for one another. We giggled and laughed for what seemed like forever before finally going to the register to check out. As we stood in line, my phone began vibrating in my purse. I decided not to answer it just because I didn't feel like digging it out of the bottom of my purse or having to search for it. If it were important, they would leave a message.

"Can't answer your phone anymore?" I heard a voice accuse from behind me. I turned to see Jessica standing there, her hand on her hip, giving me one of her famous death glares. Dina turned to look at her too, a look of confusion creasing her brow.

"Um," was all I could manage as she stood there glaring at me, waiting for a response.

"She probably didn't hear it," Dina assisted. "I mean I didn't hear anything."

"Excuse me, who are you?" Jessica responded, looking at Dina as if she'd never seen her before.

"Dina, I've known you since the eighth grade."

"I don't know a Dina," Jessica retorted, rolling her eyes and placing her focus back on me.

Share Your Thoughts

In this segment, Madison goes out with an old friend Dina and runs into an angry Jessica. After learning a little about manners, how do you think Dina handled the situation? What about Jessica? How would you have handled it if you were Madison?

SCRAPBOOK YOUR THOUGHTS

Session Six

Session Six

Pre-Activity

What do you do?

1. You're standing at the counter of a movie theatre, waiting to order a soda and popcorn. The line is extremely long and your movie starts in two minutes. The girl standing in line in front of you waves over her friends who all cut you. What do you do?

_____

_____

_____

2. You've just arrived home from school and are unpacking your books and binders out of your book bag, settling on your bed to begin your schoolwork. Tired, you removed your shoes and jacket and left it on your dresser. As you relax on your bed for a second before getting started on your homework, your mother walks in and starts yelling at you for having a "disgusting" room. What do you do?

_____

_____

_____

3. Everyday after school, you walk or ride home with the same people. Today, you know that two of those people are planning to get into a fight and they expect you to get involved. What do you do?

_____

_____

_____

4. Your mom and dad tell you that they're really proud of you for all your hard work this year and as a reward, they're going to take you and two friends to Islands of Adventure. Excited, you hurriedly tell two friends, leaving out one. Your friend who we'll name Erica who isn't chosen becomes upset and stops talking to you. In fact, she starts talking about you. What do you do?

_____

_____

_____

Session Six

Being in Public

"Be seen . . . Not heard."

1. Imagine you are walking in the mall with your mother, sister, or best friend. Recently, you had a huge birthday party so your purse is stuffed with money; around $300 to be exact. As you make your way to your favorite store, you notice a group of five boys coming towards you. It's not the size of the group that you notice first; it's their loudness. As you glance around at the other mall shoppers, you notice them watching as well. They even go as far as changing sides, getting as far away from the boys as possible. The closer they get, you can hear them cursing, insulting each other's mothers and you notice that their pants are so low, you can count the stars on one of their boxers. What are your thoughts of the group as you prepare to pass them?

   _____
   _____

   Why is it important to be seen and not heard?

2. Because how we present ourselves in **public** says:
   - How we were {shown, raised, paid}.
   - That we **care** about our {image, friends, clothes}
   - That we have **self-control.**

3. Based on our public actions, people automatically:
   - Form their {group, happiness, opinion} of you.
   - They will either **like** or **dislike** you.

- Associate you with a group of people or stereotype.

Answers: raised, image, and opinion

4. What is classified as public? (There aren't any right or wrong answers here)

A) Grocery store	E) School	H) _____
B) _____	F) Doctor's Office	I) Church
C) _____	G) Neighborhood Street	
D) Movies		

GET THE POINT?

Our public behavior says a lot about us. It shows if we have self-control, a positive self-image and the ability to know when it's a time to be loud, crazy, and fun, but also when it's not. As you can see in question four, public places are everywhere. Once you step foot out of your home, you are in public.

5. So how are you in public?

A) Are you loud? YES or NO. If you circled yes, why? Based on our lesson, how do you think people see you?

_____
_____

B) Are you in between? YES or NO. This means that you know when to be quiet and when to let it out. If you answered yes, why? Also, how do you think people see you?

_____
_____

C) Are you a quiet person? YES or NO. This means you barely make a peep. If you answered yes, is this a good or bad thing?

_____
_____

Session Six

Explore

"Jeez Jessica, why do you have to be so rude?" I asked, trying to calm the situation. "It really isn't as big of a deal as you're making it out to be. I didn't answer my phone, sorry."

"Rude?" she shouted, making everyone in the store turn and look at us. "You're the rude one. You ignore my calls and lie saying that you're grounded, but here you are . . . out shopping with Dina! Don't tell me what's a big deal. You're supposed to be my best friend, but right now you're acting like anything but that."

"Really Jessica? Do you really want to talk about someone acting like a best friend?"

"What's that supposed to mean?" she boomed.

"Could you please lower your voice?" I whispered, my face flushing red with embarrassment at the scene she was causing.

"Is everything okay?" asked the clerk who had stopped ringing up the girl in front of us and was now staring at the three of us.

"Yes," Dina answered, smiling uncomfortably. "Madison just ignore her," she said to me before turning away from Jessica.

"I think you should leave Jess. Right now you're mad and are making a huge scene. We can talk about this later."

"Later? Oh please," she spat before storming off.

My heart sank as she stormed out of the store enraged. I was totally embarrassed. The odd part was that I'm pretty sure I was more embarrassed for her than I was for myself. She was such a mess. It seemed like she was unraveling at the seams more and more each day. Just an out of control tornado, ready to destroy anything in it's path and in this instance, it's target was me.

Share Your Thoughts

Think of a time when you were in public and got totally embarrassed. Was it something you did or someone else? Explain what happened. How did it make you feel?

SCRAPBOOK YOUR THOUGHTS

Session Seven

Session Seven

Personal Appearance

"How you look, determines how you're treated."

Imagine you're at the Cheesecake Factory with your family, waiting for your table. As you lean against the wall waiting for your names to be called, a girl who looks about your age comes and stands in front of you. Your eyes widen as you notice her outfit. She has on shorts that are so short and tight that her rear end is nearly visible under the frayed denim. On top, she's wearing a black-laced camisole with a red bra peeking through. As others begin to notice her and snicker, you begin to feel bad for her.

After imagining this girl, we'll name her Jessica, what are your thoughts about her?

_____
_____

Do you think your first impression of her is actually who she really is?

_____
_____

So why is your personal appearance so important?

1. **Your personal appearance is important because:**
    A) It {sends, copies, directs} a message.
    - **negative** or **positive**.
    B) It {simplifies, draws, lessens} reactions.
    C) It **affects** how you are treated.

If you answered **sends** and **draws**, you are correct! Our personal appearance sends a message to others about us. Sometimes these messages can be positive, but they can also be negative. Ultimately, the first impression people formulate of us comes from our personal appearance or how we present ourselves. First impressions are great, but having a good personal appearance can also be beneficial for us.

2. **Having a great personal appearance is not only good for others, but for you because:**

    A) Looking {okay, good, blah} makes you **feel** good.

    B) Compliments help {boost, lower, shrink} self-esteem.

    C) People will **respect** you.

    D) Others will **look** {down, up, strangely} to you.

Answers: Good, boost, and up.

3. **What are some ways we can improve our appearance?**
    A) Keeping your hair **clean**, **combed**, and **styled**.
    B) Keeping your **nails** clean and/or **polished**.
    C) Taking **care** of your clothes.
    D) Wearing **accessories**.
    - Bracelets
    - Belts
    - Necklaces
    - Rings

E) Taking care of your **skin**.

F) Keeping your **shoes** clean for as long as possible.

5. Think about your current appearance. Based on our discussion, what are some things you can do today that would improve your appearance and help you feel great about yourself?

_____
_____

It is important to remember that having a good personal appearance is not just about others, it's about feeling good about yourself and who you are. There's nothing more important than loving yourself and the skin you're in.

Session Seven

Explore

When I arrived home from the mall, I was a little more than frustrated. I pulled all my new purchases out of the bags, laying them across the bed and taking a mental inventory. I've always loved buying new clothes, even if they were from the thrift store because they made me feel good. My parents never have a lot of money so I appreciate when I can buy something new and I always make sure I take care of what they buy me.

Picking up the purple ruffled dress I'd just purchased, I slid it on, getting ready for dinner. My parents decided it would be nice to go out for dinner since my dad made it home from work early. I thought it was a great idea because after today, I really needed to talk to my parents and get their opinion on things. I finished getting dressed and met my parents downstairs where they waited by the door.

"You look beautiful honey," my dad complimented as I reached the doorway.

"Thanks dad," I blushed, feeling an instant boost of self-esteem. It wasn't that I was obsessed with my looks or anything, but it meant a lot when I knew my dad cared to notice.

My dad treated us to seafood at one of our family's favorite restaurants. We talked about school, his work, and then the question came up . . . Jessica.

"So I haven't heard you talking about Jessica at all," my dad noted. "What happened to her?"

"Other than the fact that she's horrible?" my mom chimed in.

"Honey," my dad warned.

"Um, she's okay I guess," I lied, picking at my fish and chips.

"Okay?" my dad prompted.

"Well I saw her today and she totally flipped out on me. I feel like she's getting worse and I'm really worried about her."

"Good thing you stopped being friends with her. I told you that girl had issues."

"Mom," I groaned. "You're not really helping. As much as I don't want to be friends with her, I still think someone should try talking to her."

"I'm proud of you honey. You're absolutely right," my dad smiled. "I think you should find some time for the two of you to get together and talk if you think it's important. Maybe you can have her come over tonight and the two of you can sort things out. Just remember, in order to be effective and caring, you have to choose your words wisely."

Share Your Thoughts

What are some ways your appearance affects you? Do you think it's common to feel this way? What are some things that bother you the most? Why?

SCRAPBOOK YOUR THOUGHTS

Session Eight

Session Eight

Pre-Activity

What comes out of your mouth?

Positives   **Negatives**

For this activity, I want you to think about some of the things you've said today (or this week if you can remember that far). On the left you'll notice a column for positive words and on the right a column for negative words. Think hard about your conversations and then list as many words you can remember. You'll find out why later.

Session Eight

Choose Your Words Wisely

"What comes out of your mouth, originated in your heart."

1. Take a moment and think of something hurtful that someone said to you. It could be recent or from a long time ago. Write their comment below. How did it make you feel?

2. The hardest thing for us to control is our {hand, mouth, foot}.

- Why do you think that is?
- Are Americans more likely to use words in any way? Why?

3. As strange as it is, words hold a lot of {stuff, value, power}.

Why do you think words hold so much power?

_____
_____

Answers: mouth and power

4. Words hold power because they come from the <u>heart</u>.
   A) Sometimes their **<u>thought</u>** out.
   B) Sometimes they come out like **<u>vomit</u>**.
   C) Either way, they have the power to **<u>change</u>** someone's **<u>life</u>**.
   D) The worst thing is that we can't take our words **<u>back</u>**.

Now that we know the power of words, let's look at how we should and shouldn't use them.

5. We shouldn't use words to:
   A) Harass
   B) {Encourage, congratulate, attack}
   C) Make **fun** of others.
   D) Make others feel stupid.
   E) Most importantly, we shouldn't use words to {Sing, curse, whisper}!

6. If you curse it says:
   A) You're {Educated, uneducated, smart}.
   B) You don't care about your **personal appearance**.

As a young lady, it is very unattractive to use curse words. The more you read and learn, the bigger your vocabulary will become; giving you the ability to replace curse words with more appropriate ways to express your feelings.

Answers: Attack and uneducated

7. We should use words to:
   A) Encourage
   B) Compliment
   C) Communicate our **thoughts** and **opinions.**

How will you use your words?

_____
_____
_____
_____

Session Eight

Explore

I sat on my bed, picking at the bright purple thread of my pajama pant leg, wondering how on Earth things were going to go. My mind raced and my stomach did somersaults as I rehearsed over and over again what I wanted to say to Jessica. She would be here any minute and for some reason, my confidence was shrinking by the second. On the ride home, I mustered the courage to text her and ask her to come over. It took a little coaxing, but she finally agreed to come. I shifted uncomfortably on my white lace comforter, waiting to hear the sound of the doorbell. I couldn't imagine what was taking her so long. It's not like she lived far; it was five minutes walking at the most.

Ten minutes later, which seemed more like an hour, the bell finally rang; making me jump. The racing of my heart tripled as the voices from the living room crept up the stairs. I could hear my dad being his happy, jolly self as he greeted Jessica, making her giggle like always. My mom's voice was there, but I could tell it was one of her forced welcomes. It wasn't that my mom was a mean person because she wasn't. She was simply one of those people who could like anyone but if you gave her a reason not to like you, there was no way to go back and change her mind.

"Madison," my dad called from downstairs. "Jessica's here. Should I send her up to the dungeon?"

"Yes please," I yelled, darting across the room and whipping the door open.

Jessica appeared at the top of the stairs. Her hair was a mess of curls and her eyes seemed a little puffier than usual. If I knew anything about her, I knew when she'd been crying and it was clear she had. I took a step back, letting her into my room without saying a word. She walked past me, sitting on her favorite pink shag rug that was tucked in the corner of the room. I shut the door behind me, wondering where I should start. She looked awful and I know she knew it because instead of her usual "in your face" self, she had her head down and was concentrating on picking at the rug.

"Uh," I began, not knowing what to say. "Are you okay?" She didn't answer right away, she just kept picking at the fibers, her loose curls covering her face. "Look Jess," I continued. "I'm sorry if I made you feel bad or hurt your feelings. And yes, I shouldn't have lied but I was mad at you. Wait I take that back, I was p-oed at you."

"At me?" she finally spoke, her voice full of surprise. "What did I do to you?"

"Are you serious?" I asked, trying to keep a level voice. She nodded in response, lifting her head up and looking at me. "Honestly Jess, you've been treating me really bad. You're always asking me to do bad things, you made fun of me in front of those guys at the party . . . You know what, it doesn't even matter. I just want to make sure you're okay."

"Oh my gosh Madison, I'm so sorry. I didn't even think those things would bother you and I completely forgot about the party. I just thought you didn't want to be friends with me because you found new ones."

"Jess I would never do anything like that," I assured her, walking over and sitting cross-legged on my bed. "You're my best friend, but I can only be friends with people who make me feel better about myself, not worse."

"Yeah," she sighed, shaking her head. "I don't know what's happening to me. I used to be so 'good.' I didn't realize how bad things were getting. My parents are mad at me, you're mad at me. It just feels like I can't do anything right."

"You can do things right. You just have to make the decision to change."

"I know. So are we friends again?" she asked, a coy smile creeping onto her face.

"Sure," I smiled, leaping from my bed and giving her a hug.

Share Your Thoughts

As the story ends, Madison and Jessica make up and have a tough conversation. In the segment, we see Madison struggling to find the right words to say so she doesn't offend Jessica. Think about a time where you had to have a tough conversation. What did you have to talk about? How did it end for you?

----

www.ingramcontent.com/pod-product-compliance
Lightning Source LLC
Chambersburg PA
CBHW080447110426
42743CB00016B/3305